The rise

&

Fall of

Cleopatra II

Omar M Khayyam

Published by

BOOK DETAILS

Title	The Rise & Fall of Cleopatra II
Author's Name	Omar M Khayyam
Book Size	5.5 X 8.5
Pages	118
Published by	MIN E KAVI (மின்கவி)
Publisher details	MIN E KAVI (மின்கவி)
	(E-Development & Digital Publishing)
	www.minekavi.com
	Phone: 9626227537
Edition	I
ISBN	978-81-967424-7-8
Copyrights:	© Author

Sometimes facts are crazier than fiction.

This was what happened in the rise and fall of Jayalalithaa, the Cleopatra II. She was unique. As the first woman chief minister of Tamil Nādu, she became a nightmare even to a veteran like Karunanithi. She could fall many times but could rise from the ashes like a real phoenix. Chanakya and Machiavelli, could take a few lessons from her for the statecraft, for the shrewd moves of her coins, for the charismatic hold on the masses.

This is a thriller novel - a work of fiction with a blend of facts – how much is each, left to the readers to decide.

But you cannot put down the book

TABLE OF CONTENTS

CHAPTER 1

"Did you make the transfer to my account Madam?"

"Wait, wait, wait wherever you are. It will take a few minutes until the process is done and get reflected in your account."

He waited for some time, not nervously; He was very cool, composed and even serene.

He was intently peering at his hand held mobile which was showing a series of SMS.

Then came all of a sudden. It said an amount of 10 crore rupees had been transferred to his account in State Bank of India and the present balance was rupees ten crore, eighty thousand and twenty.

There was a call

"Is it okay? You got what you wanted... and you will send the packet today..."

"Yes Mam, I will keep my words- every bit of it; you are really a gem of a person".

"I have the packet in my hand properly sealed safe and secure. I am sending this through a special Professional Courier who does not know what it contains. The address to is yours; address "from" is a fake, fictitious one".

"He will bring to you this packet along with many other parcels being sent by many others. But please make sure that today you ask your personal assistant to bring everything straight to you – you must make sure that my packet reaches your hand. There is nothing seriously wrong if it opened by someone else. Nobody will understand what it is; most likely it will be dumped into a waste basket. But, you will not get what you wanted most. So, please take care. Only when you give me a call, affirming safe receipt I will make my next move..."

"Got it". There was a pause, an ominous silence. "Are you sure that you want to go through it...."

"Yes I am. I stand to gain every bit. Madam, I am at the edge of an abyss."

The phone went dead. After four hours, his mobile gave a mild, whimpering sound.

"I got the packet and have secured the content in some safe please..." There was a pause "Thank you".

"Okay Madam. Countdown begins from now. Good bye..."

He opened up a piece of chocolate wrapped up in two polythene papers and gently put them in his mouth. He chewed it and tasted the flavor and rich sweetened milk- death cannot be sweeter than this; he smiled – a wry smile.

Dr.Paranthaman fingered on his mobile.

"Vedamma, I am all set to take the flight to Singapore.......".

"Take care Appa, I don't know why are so keen to attend this conference. You must take care of your heart and do not stress yourself too much. Take all the medicines at right times. I will be thinking of you all the time"

"Yes ma", Paranthaman smiled a wry smile.

"I know that; but I am not so sure that if you will think of me   even after your marriage with a handsome man ,........ which will happen in a short time ....."

"Appa ...." a mumbled, demurred voice

"I know, I know; don't you worry at all. My heart is good and strong..... My only dream at this moment, Veda, is that you must get a job in the government and get married and have a nice, long happy life..."... there was a pause.

"I know, you will. I am surer about it than any other time....   Take care and good bye...."

The flight to Singapore, reached about four hours later and the air hostess found   Dr. Paranthaman, Senior Toxicologist of Tamil Nadu government, dead with a Hadly Chase novel spread out on his lap.

Later, he was found to have died of massive heart arrest, in his sleep. Singapore Air lines medical officer signed the papers and sent to General Insurance Claims.

When this news reached Jaya she read it with a twinge of pain. She felt really guilty and sad. But before this emotion could swell up and reach her head, a set of party workers, with a big fat garland, were coming towards her to facilitate on her birth day.

It was a rude shock to Veda that her father Paranthaman had died in the airplane, on his flight to Singapore. She bitterly cried for a few days; for she was all alone and her father was the only hope for her. Her mother had died about six years ago and she was a spinster at 30. Who would marry her? Who would take care of the pains of finding suitable handsome young man to take her into the wedlock?

Tamil Nadu is certainly a progressive state in terms of social structure. It is not ridden with caste or religious barrier as in Madhya Pradesh or Bihar. Yet, yet, a Kallar caste is a Kallar caste even in Tamil Nadu, in spite of the stormy petrels like EVR and Annadurai.

A few hundred years ago, when Tamil Nādu was ruled by kings – Particularly Pandya Kings in the south, these Kallars were rugged soldiers.

They were known for their dedication and valor as "body guards" (or latter day black cats of 20th century) who loved and lived with sharp swords, to protect the king.

But the kings were gone, dust unto dust and this cadre of tall, hefty, sabre - rattling body guards become all of a sudden jobless. They did not know anything except fighting in the war or occasional skirmishes. Many of them ended up as dacoits, bandits; some of them excelled as professional thieves, trained in the skills of climbing up the walls and pilfering the staked riches of landlords.

Veda was a small, insignificant chip of that caste. She was educated up to a graduate level – Bsc – Chemistry – because her father Dr.Paranthaman was a senior toxicologist in the Tamil Nadu Government Department of Community Medicine.

She was not a beauty – not an ugly duckling too; she was one of those young ladies you can see in any part of Tamil Nadu. Many of her friends, classmates, of her charm or beauty and age got married long ago, had become mother of two! But Veda remained a spinster, for she was born with "Sevva Thosam". She was born at a time when, in the celestial sphere, Jupiter, Moon and Mars were in pitched fight against each other. This was what the astrologers have found out from their accurate calculation. All those girls born under this inauspicious time would carry the stigma that any man who dared to marry her, would die young. That means, the unlucky girl would end up soon as a widow! Who would dare to marry her! There is one possible way out: If the father could find out an eligible bachelor born under the same constellation of warring Mars -Sevva Thosam – she could he married to him. This was because this bachelor also need to find out a young woman of same astrological stigma; otherwise, if this warning had been ignored, he also would lose his wife and end up as a widower. But, if a man with this stigma managed to marry a woman with the same stigma – like two negatives on multiplications becoming positive – the pair could have a normal, happy married life.

But where to find a graduate bachelor, in the Kallar caste, with the "Sevva Thosam"?. The "bandwidth" of eligible bachelor had become so narrow that Veda became a wilting, withering, fuming woman.

But all these could be wiped away by the way Dr. Paranthaman had meticulously planned.

As he died in the flight, his nominee, Veda, got substantial – about a crore rupee as insurance; She got a job in the Tamil Nādu Government as her father had died on duty; In addition, to her incredible surprise, there was an amount of ten crore rupees in her father's account. "Madam was really kind" – after all a woman knows the travails of another woman. Within next six months a young graduate who never cared all the above restrictions could squeeze his way to marry Veda.

After all, money could transcend all barriers!!

CHAPTER 2

1965 – 1987

"Who is this new actress, looking so fresh like a bloom of a rose..."

It was spontaneous blurt from the great MGR on seeing Jaya for the first time in a movie production set.

The hero asked the producer Panthulu. This one question was enough for the latter. He could see the glitter in eyes of the hero, the super hero, the Puratchi Nadigar (Revolutionary Actor) MGR and he knew that MGR's heart and head had started melting. Also, he could sense that these two would pair up not only in movies, but in private life for many years to come. But he would have never dreamt, even in the craziest, queerest, wild dreams that this young vivacious actress of age seventeen would become the Queen of Tamil Nadu.

Years rolled on and they were rolling on together in real life and celluloid lives.

Jaya never expected that she would be brought so close to the matinee idol MGR. His fair complexion, the fairest she has ever seen till her young age of 18, the gentle smile flowing down his lips, all gave a pleasant shock in her. The shock was rather mutual, for only after many years, MGR had come across such a lovely girl; May be years ago when Saroja Devi was the heroine in one of his movies, he had seen such a beauty; but that was almost fifteen years ago! They never could have imagined that each one would have a decisive role in the destiny of others. What was more, both, individually, and collectively wrote the history of Tamil Nadu.

Jaya was very reluctant to enter the tinsel world of movies. She would have preferred to be a dancer, or a lawyer or a school teacher with ravenous hunger for books. She had a quick wit, a razor –sharp brain which galloped across the situation and took a firm grasp of the future course of action. Over and above, she had an inherent charm and poise. What could have enamored MGR was the elegant English that danced at the tip of her tongue. He had never seen, before or after, anyone who could go close to her in the agility of thoughts or expression. Though she had a occasions to act as a heroine over 100 movies, with many super stars of her time, she made the best pair with MGR.

This brought lot of wealth and fame for Jaya; but not so much for MGR, for he had already become a super hero in Tamil movies. Perhaps because of this, Jaya wanted to be closer and closer to MGR, almost at the level of feeling possessive.

When her mother passed away, there was none, except MGR, for Jaya to lean upon at times of stress and frustrations.

"Amma, Amma, ... She cried like a school girl because, she had a checkered life with her happy-go-happy father and cine actress mother. And now she was no more all of a sudden.

"Don't you worry at all; death is natural; everyone must die one day. But unfortunately, your mother is too young to die. Strangely that is the way of God or Nature 's game ..."

MGR was patting her Jaya. There was immense personal warmth. She was only twenty-four and he fifty-five, the age of her father.

This made her deeply emotionally attached towards MGR On many of such times, she could lean on a stalwart like MGR. Their relation was an odd, distorted convolution of paternal tenderness turning into a kind of amour! Love is crazy and it can find its own routes!

From the first movie Ayirathil Oruvan, MGR became a hero, one in thousand; and Jaya unacknowledged "girlfriend", only one of its kind!

M.G.R. was also equally possessive; in the next two decades or so, they were climbing up the stairs of success and fame. Other male actors, including even the stalwarts like Sivaji, were slowly snapped off from Jaya-very gently, very unobtrusively, but very definitely. For Jaya, the "Puratchi Thalaivar" was a role model, a guardian angel, a father figure, and strange lover, all rolled into one.

Things would have gone like this and both would have lived, loved and acted for a few more years and died unsung and unnoticed. At the best they would have been honored with two obituary notices in all major newspapers (something like this happened for Gemini Ganesh and Savitri!) but for one, only one person, Mr. Karunanidhi fondly and respectfully known as Kalaignar Karunanidhi.

Kalaignar never wanted to make MGR a hero of Tamil Nadu politics, nor a heroine out of Jaya. But he did it, unwittingly, unexpectedly. "There are more things in heaven and earth than are dreamt off in your philosophy Mr. Karunanidhi".

Jaya would have a few tens or tons of opportunities to say out this for the next few decades.

MGR and Kalaignar were good friends; and for many of the hit movies of MGR, Kalaignar was the script and dialogue writer, in which he excelled himself and had carved out an enviable niche. Not even five percent of the movies were flops in which MGR was a hero; or Kalaignar had penned the script.

Apart from the talents in cine-field, Kalaignar and MGR both were tall figures in Dravidian movement in Tamil Nādu, which was sweeping across the sixties and seventies. When in 1967, DMK, won the election and CN Annadurai, the DMK leader became the chief Minister, the whole of Tamil Nadu felt a resurgence, rejuvenation. But within a year the chief minister passed away and in the inner-party, subdued struggle, Karunanidhi became the Chief minister of Tamil Nadu, with a strong support by MGR.

Things were going smoothly, between the two titans for quite some time; but then they started to fall out of steps, for each was a titan, and each had an ego of Hercules.

"Power corrupts and absolute power corrupt absolutely" is the saying common in politics. It cannot be truer than with Karunanidhi. After a few years, Kalaignar started to hold up all the strings in his hands. Party men, smaller and bigger, started fuming and fretting. At some point of time the eruption and fission came in the form of MGR starting up a new party called the All India Anna DMK (AIADMK).

Note, in 1967, it was a tough tussle between the Congress party and fledgling DMK. The Congress party, which ruled Tamil Nadu over 20 years, was over thrown by

DMK, making use of the very popular upheaval of Anti – Hindi Agitation.

In 1977, MGR became the Chief Minster (CM)of Tamil Nadu. That was in five years since 1972, when he was sacked out – not kicked out – of DMK. MGR could gather enormous momentum to capture the power from the stalwart like Mr. M Karunanidhi.

What was stranger, that MGR could seize – not the pound of flesh – but the whole flesh – from the mouth of the lion in five years. There was no great political issue that MGR brought forth against Karunanidhi; it was just his charisma!

He was a hero in the movie, savior of poor and sick. So, he must be the savior in real life too! MGR seemed to have stepped out of the white screen of the theatre to comfort and console the down trodden – No, he has come down as an "Avatar" to solve the issues, to uplift the poor. The demi – God of celluloid world became the real god of real life. So, thought the Tamil

"It is a strange phenomenon" wrote the editor of a an elite newspaper " the elite, intellectual and cultural capital of India, has elected a cine actor as the Chief Minister of the state" It is indeed a rare phenomenon, that a full -fledged cine actor, who was living in the tinsel world of din and noise, music and make -beliefs could convince the big masses of voters that he would be a "redeemer", a super hero ,giving sucker to sick ladies, in real life, as much as in celluloid screens.

MGR was CM of Tamil Nādu? No... he was the king of Tamil Nadu.; this was how Jaya felt, perceived. She gave him a big sword, worthy of a king, to the sabre -rattling celluloid hero.

By making him a king, she made herself a queen. In due course, she became AIADMK propaganda secretary, and then an MP. Should not her mellifluous English resonate in the galleries of parliament in Delhi?

Two important moves by MGR that propped up Jaya into the forefront in the politics jungle war- fare.

In 1987, there was the big government organized "World Tamil Conference" in which Jaya performed a dance and she won the title "The Gift of Cauvery". This put her in the lime light among the partymen and all down the ladders.

The next one was the implementation of "Nutritious Meal" to all the school children in Tamil Nadu. It was a sequel to Kamaraj's "Mid- noon meal scheme", which was a roaring success. The whole of Tamil Nadu felt indebted to this CM, Mr Kamaraj as a demigod, or great leader who brought school education to the homes of every village and wayward urchins.

What MGR did was to push it up to be a better nutritious rich food supply chain in the midnoon.

When Jaya was given a free hand to run the show, run the scheme into an effective implementation by the government machinery, MGR and Jaya both became important luminaries in the galaxy of politics too. Two stars from the virtual field had jumped out the screen to become real stars in politics, to save the poor.

Then on, MGR and Jaya were almost inseparable in movies and life too, each was possessive of the other. Yet, there was an army of admirers of MGR who kept striking wedges between MGR and Jaya. Because of these coteries and manipulations, the two were blowing hot and cold.

It was during this period , Jaya had a chance to get to know about Soban Babu , a Telugu actor . Perhaps they were "dating" occasionally.

Soban Babu came close and tangentially ran off or cringed away from Jaya. It was a heart – rending frustration for her. The cold disappointment had   frozen into silent volcano in the heart of Jaya.

It was said that the tip off to "keep away from my dear Ammu" was said to have come from MGR.

If only MGR had not "tipped off", if only the marriage between Soban Babu and Jaya had taken place, the history of Tamil Nadu had to be rewritten.

In Cleopatra 's life she came across two heroes: Julius Caesar and then Antony, one after another. In Jaya's also two heroes, alternatingly and almost simultaneously; but alas, none matured up into anything to worth reminiscing!!

Both were fast – touch – and – go. She never had come across in her life any young, jolly, happy – go – lucky hero with whose she could dance in the gardens and fly in the clouds, as she had done in the cinema field.

The two men whom she came quite close were married, middle aged men and their relation with her was only second – hand, half – hidden.

All these had instilled little by little a kind of inveterate hatred against MANkind! For the rest of her life, when she became the CM of Tamil Nadu, men could feel the controlled but seething anger on them. She was really the Queen and all ministers were just pawns, knights etc. with no king in her chess board.

For a few years, even for a decade, there was a hot and cold war between the army of Jaya haters and Jaya. She was able to hold at bay, the whole team, something a tiger holding a pack of hungry wolves.

She had the steely nerves; she had the guts and ferocity. The team of "Jaya haters" helped her to sharpen her sword to face the Goliath, Mr Karunanidhi for next two decades.

When the king and queen lived happily in all majesty and grandeur, envy is expected to erupt. It did; particularly so, when MGR had to go to USA for some serious treatment. Jaya was half dead. Many of her enemies were hatching up plots after plot to make her full dead. But somehow, she could wriggle out and escape in to wilderness.

In 1977, when MGR became the chief minister, MGR and Jaya knew each other over twelve years. And this tenure was more than enough for a lady with an incisive acumen to gauge and judge the strengths and weakness of her "boy" friend, the "mentor", the "icon".

Within a few months, Jaya could meet a host of pawns, knights, bishops of the political chess game. She could see that many of them were ill-educated, power hungry, ill manned. Money was the only one route, royal route to the political power; and the political power was the only route to rule the masses.

She was self-conscious of two very invaluable weapons she had: she was shrewd; and she was a graceful, beautiful women. This was a very rare combination; and like a double – barrel cannon, it could demolish many forts.

When a woman stands before a man – watch out any man – he is only half-strong; when she is beautiful and lovely, he is quarter – strong; when she is charming and intelligent, man, is almost a zero!

This was what Cleopatra had about two thousand years ago. After a long gap, Jaya had a double helix of sharp acumen and charisma.

She became the Cleopatra of Tamil Nadu and MGR the Antony who could neither accept her as the heir of his throne or throw her out as an upstart usurper. Before he could choose any one option, he breathed his last.

This was a crazy slant destiny written on Tamil Nadu.

"Amma!!!!! puratchi thalaivar is dead..." Some body screamed and cried in her drawing hall. It came like a bolt from the blue. She reeled under the shock, but bounced back, she rushed into the crowd where MGR's dead body was being carried away in procession.

"Here comes the wretch, the wench, here comes his bed-mate"

"Okay, okay she can sleep with him now"

All these words hit her with poisoned arrows; yet Jaya swallowed them and digested all of them. As she was trying to climb up the funeral cart, she was kicked down, her saree was pulled off. No, No, No, Jaya was dying in shame and insult but she was not dead.

When MGR's body was laid in honor in Rajaji Hall, she could somehow manage to squeeze herself into the crowd and stand guard near his body. Her legs were trampled upon; some dirty hands groped into her body. Yet she swallowed all the insult in subdued rancor. It was on this day at this humiliating moment, she visualized that someday, her dead body also would lie-in-state in the same place, with the same state-honor.

She would make sure of it, for she was a woman, made of steel nerves, who wrote her diary- no , no who wrote her destiny!!

CHAPTER 3

1989- 2001

"Get her, get her out" Jaya screamed at the intrusion. She was walking back and forth in her chamber, a spacious personal room. Jaya was a wounded lion, a deserted fox, sauntering here and there. She was never more disappointed, never more mortified.

She heard the news that Janaki Ramachandran, a quiet, sick widow of the late chief minister MGR had been propped up and sworn in as the next CM, by a coterie of strong men in the AIADMK. It was a hushed, rushed, and clandestine operation concocted around to prevent Jaya wielding any power in the party.

Jaya was restless to the point of breakdown to tears. For all her dreams of becoming secretary to the great party, as a strong person, next only MGR in power and adulation, all got shattered in a jiffy. She did not know what to do; there was no one – not a weak or strong soul- to give a trace of clue to come out this debacle.

The servant maid brought her cup of coffee. She was scared to look at the Madam, whose face was livid and eyes reddish.

"Madam, there is a lady waiting to meet you. She says it is urgent and important".

"Who is she.......?

"She is the one who brings audio and video cassettes to you as and when you want them. She owns a video cassette shop nearby. She is very insistent. I tried to chase her out- but she gave a small envelope and asked you to just open and read what is inside..."

Jaya casually tore open the envelope and there was a small white piece of paper, in which there were only three words:

"Secrets of Janaki"

That was it. Jaya froze and asked the maid to bring the lady upstairs.

Kanchana, a graceful young lady, aged around 25 or 30, entered into the chamber of Jaya. It is a kind of symbolic "Walk-in" into the life of Jaya.

"Who are you"

"What is your name?"

"Where are you coming from and ...."

"Madam, we are all disappointed very much like you, when you have not become a CM. Instead, an unknown, decrepit woman has usurped your place ...... your throne.

"Who are you?......."

"I am an ordinary fan of ADMK and a great fan of you not only as a cine actress, but as a promising, smart political leader who had been chosen and shaped by the Puratchi thalaivar to succeed him..."

"Who are you, where are you from "

"I am Kanchana, native of Thiruppangili, near Trichy..... and I have a video cassette shop, within easy reach from here.... Give me only one more minute... my husband Seetharam is the personal secretary of Janaki, the wife of MGR and he was coughing out so many secrets unknown to the world. This is not the first time that he spills out the beans. On many occasion, in bed, in high pitch of romantic moods, he would say that he knows so many secrets that would rock the world."

"This is what the men would say, in bed, in high romance, to impress upon the wife. I never cared a wee bit all along; but somehow, what he said yesterday night, got stuck in my heart, and I thought I could share with you......"

"Sit down in this chair Kanchana.. Am I right"

There was a kind of softness, gentleness in the voice.

Kanchana sat down; very polite, very docile.

"Yes go ahead; what do you want to say about Madam Janaki....."

"Can I be open and frank......"

"Yes, go ahead....."

"Madam Janaki is dying. She has some kind of disease, some kind of blood cancer. She has been taking strong medicine and according to my husband, her days are numbered... may be a month or two.. not more....

"What, What?!

"Yes mam. We know for sure that she has serious health issue and may not pull along   for long. She never wanted to be a CM or anything. Once her dear husband MGR has been dead, she wished she was dead too."

There was a pause. Words and their implications were slowly sinking into Jaya.

"For her, nothing exists beyond her husband. All these swearing in as CM, state honor all look like crazy "dhamasha" She had been brainwashed by Samiyappan and Raghunathan into accepting this chief minister position .... She knows that she would be just a puppet in the hands of this band of elected "bandits". They don't know that she would not live beyond a few months; but they don't care wee bit. For them this is the best time to coerce, brainwash, buy all the MLAs to dance to the tune of this duo... to usurp and rule party and the state."

Kanchana stopped at this point. She wanted the implication of her "revelation" to percolate slowly into Jaya's mind.

"Okay, thank you..." Jaya came close and took out a nice gold chain from her neck and garlanded on Kanchana.

"You can go and leave your phone number with the maid... and I will call you if and when necessary."

"Thank you Mam. I will cherish your love. Maybe you can talk to my husband, who is many times more informed and more intelligent. He knows, everything and everybody in MGR's ministry.

"Okay. Okay Thank You... for now."

Kanchana was about to leave.

"Who is your husband? I mean what is he and how does he know all these?"

"Madam, my husband Seetharam is the personal secretary to Madam Janaki for last ten years. He is her cousin brother, and above all he is her only confidante, only trustworthy person"

As Kanchana left the hall and walked through the drawing room, towards the gate, Jaya called her personal assistant to follow her.

"Follow this lady like a shadow. Get all the information, every bit and bring to me in ten hours. Now it is ten morning and meet me at eight in the evening. I need to know every scrap of reliable information about her and her husband.... all very discretely. Neither she, nor her husband could ever sniff a trace of our exploration."

The information came in after ten hours, through her personal detective

"Yes, she is a video shop vendor; Her name is Kanchana, aged 28, married to one Mr. Seetharaman aged 32, a middle level government officer, deputed as a PA3 for the CM."

"He is expected to be at the beck and call of MGR or his wife Janaki. His office is a small building at hundred meters away from main house in Ramavaram Gardens. He and one or two security men would drive their car, "piloting", or forerunning, when Madam goes to shopping, which is rare, or hospital, which is quite frequent. Theirs is a small, middle-class family and there is nothing special or worth mentioning."

Next day Kanchana had a phone call from the madam Jaya. She was required to meet her in two hours, along with her husband.

When Seetharam came in and opened up a treasure house of information about MGR and Janaki, and the whims and vagaries of host of ministers in the newly formed Government with Janaki Ramachandran as the CM, Jaya knew how to chip off the ministry. The whole picture of what would happen in next two years, she could see, vividly like a crystal gazing magician.

In the next few weeks, the Tamil Nadu Assembly met and created history as the most riotous meets, of all time. Chairs, books, mikes were hurled at each other and the speaker of the Assembly, unilaterally, perhaps, substantially 'oiled with money" declared that the CM Janaki had won the required vote of confidence. But the Governor, who received the whole report through his secretaries recommended for the dissolution and fresh mandate.

Now the battle lines were drawn: The party had a vertical split: on one side, people saw the old wife, old friends, old wire pullers and the other side, a young glamorous cine actress who had the charm and grace of a modern lady.

Have you ever seen the fight between an elephant and tiger? Elephant is many times heavier, stronger and bigger than the tiger. But tiger is faster, swifter, agile and ferocious. So was Jaya.

She travelled east and west, north and south of Tamil Nadu; spoke to the common people particularly the womenfolk and "begged" for their support.

She was able to convince the people -particularly the large segment of women of villages that Jaya would be the only person who was closest to MGR and only she could carry the scepter of MGR and the AIADMK party forward against all the stemming tides of Karunanidhi, the sworn enemy of MGR. Mrs Janakai Ramachandran , with due respect for her , was just a puppet in the hands of a band of bandits who were after the power of and pelf of the Tamil Nādu government Nothing could be more true, as the next twenty years showed.

In spite of the whirlwind tour and intense emotional appeal, Jaya's party – or her part of the ADMK-could win only 27 seats . Of course, she was elected as an MLA with thumping margin of votes. The only solace was her adversary, the erstwhile CM, the erstwhile wife of MGR, had a stunning defeat. The poor, propped lady could not impress upon the voters. Not only that, most of her part of AIADMK contestants lost their deposits ; only a handful survived.

"Akka, can I tell you something...

"Yes go ahead...".

"If you don't get angry, I will say, or suggest something. This will change your fate. Of course, you might hit me in my face if I tell you this. Still I want tell you..."

"What is this"...

"We can arrange for a meeting between you and Janaki Madam..."

"What, what nonsense you talk"

"I know you will become furious but lend me your ears only for one minute. If we can arrange for this meeting, it is our responsibility to see that Janaki Madam quits politics, on some health reason. She would announce that the scepter of MGR will be carried by you. This means, if everything goes well, and it should as there is no other option- you will move into the AIADMK offices as the leader in about a month."

Jaya looked askance at Kanchana; she could not trust her. If things go as Kanchana had said, Jaya said to herself that, she would not trust anyone but Kanchana.

"Are you kidding....

"No Madam, I mean what I say. You didn't know Janaki Madam. But I know her strength and weakness; and you don't know my strength. Trust me. Permit me to take up this task. If things go well, trust me and I will be with you as your sister; If not, I will not enter into this house....."

After twenty-four hours, Seetharaman and Kanchana came up to the house in Poe's Garden. Their faces were beaming delights.

"Janaki Madam has agreed to meet you."

"When and where"

"Tomorrow she is ready to meet you. But this must be kept a closed secret. A top secret. You can go to meet her in MGRs residence in Ramapuram",

A sharp slap flashed across Kanchana's face

"No never"

"I am the winning part of the ADMK. With 27 MLA in my wing. She is the loser of the party, almost every MLA of her wing lost deposit. They were all busted to dust."

"Get out, get out," Jaya screamed as a wild cat.

"Akka..."

"Get out, get out....." Jaya screamed like a wild cat.

For next twenty-four hours, there was hectic "horse trading". The three MLAs of Janaki wing got lured into

Jaya's side for some hefty payment; slowly and gently they slipped into Jaya's "bag". Janaki's men left her all alone like a marooned catamaran.

Kanchana had a phone call from Jaya Akka by mid noon.

"Did you see what had happened. All those tiny clowns of that wings have moved into my camp.   I am ready to meet her. She must bring the keys, seals, all the accounts, and cheque books of the AIADMK party. I am AIADMK.

Thalaivar had handed over the party to me a few months ago; and now the Tamil Nādu people have handed it over to me. I am the AIADMK. Go and bring her!...." She was exulting like a Moghul empress, ------no emperor

"Okay Madam, we obey whatever you say. Even if you ask me and my wife to jump out of this balcony, we will do without thinking twice. ...". Seetharaman said.

"One small suggestion, though....... Can I say Akka...."

"What is it." The words came soaked in hot air of irritation.

"Akka, now the situation is clear. Everybody in the party feels that you are the leader, why, you are the party: you are the AIADMK. Even Ramappan and Sathappan of Janaki, the two devils, have realized this in the heart of their hearts.

It is the best time that you must go there and meet her as she is elder to you. She is the wife of our thalaivar.... This news will flash across all our party

cadres and grassroot workers, many of them women. Your gesture will be taken as a mark of nobility and grandeur."

"Madam, there is a couplet in Thirukural...." "Seetharam interjected.

"What is it ?"

"To press ahead and fight against the enemy is the mark of valor. But to be kind to the defeated is the sign of grandeur."

There was silence – an ominous tickling of seconds

"Okay, arrange for a meeting. I will go to Ramavaram Garden to meet her and share my condolences of bereaved Thalaivar...

"That is all what we want; the rest we shall take care .."

Suddenly Kanchana moved forward and kissed in the cheeks of Jaya...

In few hours, by 8pm in the evening, the finale came up.

Kanchana and Jaya were in the car gently moving into Ramavaram Gardens Seetharaman was waiting, all alone, in the gate. The only security at the gate was a Nepali, who would never know any CM or PM or DM. For him, two ladies were sitting in the car and entering into the house and Seetharaman Saheb was ushering them in.

In the hall, Janaki Madam, the widowed, withered, wilted lady was sitting.

As Jaya stepped in, she folded her hands and said "Vanakkam"

Janaki was welcoming her with open arms. As they came closer, they hugged each other and they cried bitterly and in the tears all the ego, all the pride, all the aversion and hatred got washed away. They lost themselves in their common love for their common hero. They became just two women, in whom a man had shared his love; in whom they shared their dreams.

You may say anything and everything about this swash – buckling hero, MGR; but he must have been a loving, caring man.

Janaki came forward and hugged Jaya and the latter leaned on her shoulder and cried bitterly.

Janaki was the first to recover. She led Jaya by hand to a big life-size photograph of MGR. Both bent down with folded hands and prostrated in obedience.

Then Janaki, gave a bunch of boxes, full of documents, seals, money of the party

She whimpered "I lived happily with this great man and I will now die happily since you will carry forward all his dreams......"

Jaya left the hall, with tears filling her eyes and emotions swelling up in her heart. She felt like having taken bath in the Ganges of exalted feelings.

When they reached home, It was almost eleven in night. She felt totally exhausted. She put all the treasures in her personal locker and locked them up.

"Thank you Kanchana" Jaya felt very happy; she kissed Kanchana in her cheeks. Kanchana too was very happy. There was a kind of big relief, a sense of triumph; she returned the kisses too eagerly, with a tint of passion.

Now the lines were drawn for the big battle between David and Goliath.

Now that the entire AIADMK party was with her, with official recognition, even by the Election commission of India, her only foe was Karunanithi. He was certainly formidable, nothing less than a Hercules or Goliath. This was because Karunanidhi was the undisputed leader for three decades for all the Dravidian community. He was a seasoned administrator, undefeated legislator, above all a scholar par excellence in Tamil literature. When he spoke the idiots and the erudite scholars stood in rapt attention. Against him was Jaya, a lady, a Brahmin, that too a Kannadiga Brahmin, though she had strong links in Srirangam Iyengar families.

'She would be wiped away in few years. She has managed to win some twenty odd seats because of the lingering memory of the cine- hero MGR. All these would be easily wiped off, stamped off, by the Dravidian legion, who constituted about eighty percent of the voters'. So thought Karunanithi, and all the political pundits, at that time but they were all woefully mistaken.

Jaya became the opposition leader and Karunanidhi, the CM.

"Not a day should pass in the Assembly without arguments, accusations and even disruption.

"Karunanidhi 's seat must become a hot stove!! He must never be allowed dream, sleep, not even nap, for a while"

This is the spoken, unspoken, written and unwritten law that came down from the Mount of Poe's garden.

In the first week of her participation in the Tamil Nadu assembly itself, Jaya threw a bombshell that her telephones had been tapped and the CM must be held responsible for this undemocratic process. Her party numbers raised such a hue and cry that the assembly session had to be adjourned. When it met again, chaos got doubled up.

The party members of DMK and AIADMK, were fighting with words, though not with swords. In the melee, Karunanidhi said something pretty bad to the effect that Jaya would better go and live with her lover Shoban Babu, instead of loitering the Assembly.

This led to volcanic eruption and in the free- for all melee: Karunanidhi was pushed away, he almost fell down, lost his spectacles; Jaya was also pushed down. Some crazy DMK MLA went to the extent of pulling her saree off to the utter shock and humiliation of Jaya. All these ugly scenes were being telecast alive, allover India and the viewers got the shock of their lives.

"Is it that the plight of Panchali of Mahabharatha being enacted all over again in the court of Karunaanidhi. Is he a Kalaignar or Duryothana or Dutchathana?"

Jaya came out in tears, with an inveterate vengeance, of Panchali of twentieth century, that she would dethrone the indefatigable veteran Karunaanidhi. Nothing -nothing should and would stop her until she became the CM of Tamil Nadu.

That day when Jaya returned home she locked herself in her room for a long time. Everybody outside her room were anxious and were waiting, twitching their fingers. But she came out a few hours later with livid, hardened face; maybe she had been bracing her nerves and bones with steel and concrete; may be the spirits of Chanakkiya and Panchali have found right shelters in her heart.

Do you believe in astrology?

I do not; many of you may or may not. Jaya never gave a damn if you or I believed it. She did, intently. She was born under the constellation of something called Magam. Her astrologers told her that since "you were born

under this constellation you are destined to rule the world
– at least Tamil Nadu, or even India".

Jaya did the first and tried hard for the second but
failed by a narrow slip, somewhere.

When she came out the portals of the assembly of
Tamil Nadu, with disheveled hair, bruised hands, but
hardened heart, she swore that she would step into this
hall only as a Chief minister (CM) of Tamil Nādu

Perhaps the seething volcanic eruption from her
must have reshuffled all the stars in the galaxy as the
subsequent events showed, way beyond the wildest dream
of JJ or MK(Mr M Karunaanidhi).

The dew drop of Tamil Nadu was Sri Lanka or
Ceylon. For decades, there were ethnic issues between
two natives: the majority Sinhalese and the minority (12%)
Tamils.

Such strives were nothing new. Jews were kicked
out because they were head and shoulder above the native
Egyptians. Palestinians   are   being   bombed   out   of

surrounding domains of Israel so that Jews have a bigger land mass for their country.

This time it was between the Sri Lankan army and LTTE, under the leadership of indomitable Prabhakaran, for the cause Tamils and equitable, fair rule of the law. Since India had a strong sphere of influence upon Sri Lanka, the only nearest neighbor in the sea, it sent its force to restore peace in the island. The so-called Indian Peace Keeping Force (IPKF), instead of restoring peace, quelled the strength of Tamil Revolutionaries and in this process, they had gone to the extent of causing atrocities on women.

All these spilled over into Tamil Nadu where different segments of the revolutionaries could find refuge. And they quarreled among themselves, with the shoot-outs in the streets of Chennai.

All these were brought to the forefront by JJ and she claimed – no – she roared that Mr.MK was a traitor and trying to form Ealem, a separate Tamil Nadu with north-eastern part of Sri Lanka as a tail piece. This incurred the wrath of the ruling Central government of India which dismissed DMK government citing the reason that the law and order was thrown to winds in Tamil Nadu and hence the then DMK government also should go with the wind.

In the subsequent election DMK would have been returned to power with thumping majority as JJ was just a fledgling in the party politics and she had enough foes among her team itself.

Then something happened. All the stars of JJ got aligned in a straight line forming a vector addition, that Mr. Rajiv Gandhi, former PM, got assassinated in Tamil Nadu by a band of Sri Lankan revolutionaries.

This turned the whole Tamil voters against Mr.Karunanidhi. The only alternative was not Congress, not BJP, not Communists – only JJ.

CHAPTER 4

1991 - 1996

"I, Jayaraman Jayalalitha, take the oath in the name of God, as the Chief Minister of Tamil Nadu, to uphold the constitution, to serve the people, honestly, truthfully to the best of my knowledge and efforts ...."

The day was 24 July 1991. This was the day of reckoning for her and also for Tamil Nadu!

How did she win the election?

For some of them, the main adversary Kalaignar M Karunanidhi (MK), has three wives; whereas this woman, who stood close to our great MGR, has sacrificed her life for the party of MGR. In the image of Jaya, they could see MGR. Over and above when Jaya moved into the crowd, many women came close to her, see her beauty, smell her charm. Note, that fifty percent of the voters were women and fifty percent of the women of Tamil Nadu have not gone beyond the school education and eighty percent of them would not have gone beyond their home town or village. They provided the solid, bulwark for Jaya the next twenty-five years, however corrupt Jaya and her coterie were. Because, they voted against male chauvinism. She was the incarnation of an outraged woman, a Kali, to keep the men, not under her thumb, but under her toes!

This was how the literate, semi-literate, illiterate, village woman could visualize, when they voted for Jaya for the first time and it did really happen. Watch out : even the wives of MK could have voted for JJ!!!

Immediately after the first oath taking ceremony as the CM of Tamil Nadu as she walked out, the team of ministers, fell straight prostrated at her feet, one after another, vying with each other. Not only that, after sometime during her second or third tenure as CM, when she used to fly in a helicopter, a few of the ministers would "worship" her helicopter raising their hands as much as they could. In Hindu religion, in Vaishnavite tradition, when an eagle would be flying across the sky, many devout Vaishnavas would pray with utter, dedication and their mouths would mumble or chant" Narayana, Narayana". Because sighting an eagle, the carrier bird of Lord Vishnu, was equivalent to sighting the Lord Vishnu himself. Such utter superstition had got percolated into utter servility into the AIADMK ministers.

She was careful enough to select the members of her ministry; most of them: rich, power hungry, excelling in extortion of significant amount in PWD,

Foreign investments and even in universities; above all they were utterly devoid of any independent thinking. Any minister, exhibiting some traces of smartness and clear – headedness would lose his job, before he reached his office from his home! Much less need be said about the women ministers!

"Power corrupts and absolute power corrupts absolutely" is the cliché in politics.

Jaya epitomized it.

Between 1991, when she became the CM, and the next election of 1996, she had made four major achievements – rare and daring ones : The so called cradle baby scheme which encouraged mothers of unwanted pregnancies- for whatever reasons that could have happened – the babies were accepted as the responsibilities of the state; "you just bring your burdensome baby in the midnights or early mornings; drop it in the cradle kept near temples and churches, mosques or parks and just disappear into the thin air ; that was all . It was not a movie or drama scene; It was real and it brought tears in the eyes of Mother Theresa who visited Jaya's home and blessed it.

Then came the All-women police stations. There were hundreds of real atrocities done by the men police in the police station on women (dragged in for petty crimes like pick pocketing, street scuffles, etc). It was a real revolutionary move which has led to 10 to 20 % women police force throughout Tamil Nadu, which was copied down by other states subsequently.

Then came All- women libraries, child care centers, elementary schools, ration shops etc.

She went on a fasting "until death" forcing the Union government and Karnataka state to release water in Cauvery for the benefit farmers of delta regions.

A case in point, to be singled out, was the 64% reservation, which made a big jolt in Tamil Nadu politics.

The story needs a little background to understand the implication. Dravida Kalazham (DK) was the party which evolved out of Justice Party (JP), in the twenties and thirties of the last century, during the British Rule of India. The main agenda JP or DK was a strong opposition to the Brahmin community. The total percent of Brahmin population in India was not more than 10%; yet 90% of the jobs in the government, banks, universities were all in hands of the Brahmins.

The most important reason was that the non-Brahmins were kept out of educational mainstream. They were left to fend for themselves in grocery shops, agriculture, or cleaning streets. This was a big imbalance, a gross social injustice, that had been perpetrated for a few centuries. Mr EVR Periyar, the stormy a petrel, spent all his lifetime to restore the balance. He was ready to live with the British tyranny than with the Brahminical tyranny.

DMK and its sub -set AIADMK parties were just off-shoots from the same JP and DK with the same set of ideologies. Since they hated Brahmins, they hated Vedas, Sanskrit, astrology, superstitions and all pantheons of Gods worshipped by the Brahmins.

Under this hot, humid ambience, Brahmins made exodus to the UK first and then to the USA, rather silently, seeking safer and greener pastures.

When Periyar was alive, every Brahmins had a cloud of fears above his head up above his coiled "Kudimis" (lock of hair tuft).

When Periyar died, Anna and his close associate Kalaignar Karunanithi (MK) came to power; but Brahmins have lost the fear of atrocities. But they had few options of openings in government jobs. Instead of 95% of job opportunities under the British Regime, they had only 10% now. Within these 70 years of Independence the so- called Dravidian model, had raised the educational, technical skills of the non-Brahmin community that Brahmin were wriggling in their hot seat – note, not stove.

The story may be reminiscent of what happened to the Jews under Hitler's regime, but not quite,

Because, there was no violence at all against Brahmin community. Just, they were nudged out of their prime importance, in every walk of lives. The only exclusive domain left for them was, the priesthood in many big temples, or conducting auspicious ceremonies, with Vedic rituals, in temples, in marriage or after a few days of any death (not in death beds or grave yards as in Christianity or Islam!!).

Under this hot, sultry cloud hanging above her head, Jaya, a Srirangam Iyengar Brahmin came to the power, as Queen of AIADMK, a Dravidian Party. What was more, Mr Veeramani, the disciple and DK leader came all the way to support Jayalalitha, ignoring the hue and cry from a host of his followers, because it was Jaya who ensured 64% job opportunities exclusively for non - Brahmins. Thus, she had become the savior of the non-Brahmins, the Guardian Angel of Social Justice.

Yes, she indeed did many good government measures, with immense good will – as an Amma – a mother. She was even portrayed as "Mother Mary", "Adi Parasakthi" (the prime Goddess)

Also she did two major blunders: one was her brazen holy bath in Kumbagonam Maha Magam and other was the exhibitionistic, outrageous wedding of her adopted son Sudhakaran.

First one was because of her blind faith in her astrologer's advice. A person born under the auspicious star constellation of "Magam", should take bath -a sacred dip-, in Kumbagonam Temple Maha Magam tank to ensure long and glorious life. This Maha Magam, this level of a grand constellation of Magam stars, occurred only once in twelve years. Jaya was preached and brainwashed that it was exclusively, especially suited for grand personality like her.

Jaya and her shadow sister Kanchana both took a dip holding their hands together; they even exchanged heavy garlands – something that only husband and wife would do in Indian traditions. This shocked the world, as the whole event was telecast by all TV channels.

This shock was humbled by the live telecast of scores of people dying "alive" under the very nose and eyes of the "Amma", the chief minister of the state.

A large members of villagers had come all the way to Maha Magam, this time not out of piety, but out of curiosity to see and touch the cine star of hundred movies!

A building on which hundreds were perching like crows and doves gave way and killed a few dozen and the following stampede took care of another few more dozens!

Jaya was shocked; expressed her concern. That was all. She was not anguished. She was cold blooded and cold - not cool- headed!

The next major blunder was in 1995. The incredible lavish wedding: All of a sudden, again perhaps by the advice of some astrologers or family purohits, she adopted a man of twenty - five as her son!

Up to now, it was a tolerable stupidity. But, for a person, who was a nondescript a few months ago, she organized a grand, wedding. It was not the talk of the town; but of the whole world.

Jaya and her shadow Kanchana, decked in glittering gold from their forehead to foot toes, walked a few miles in glitter and glare to the envy of everybody. The police, the administrative officials, the government vehicles all were under her mercy. She was the queen – the Queen of Tamil Nadu. She ambled in regal splendor and the expense for this was supposed to be 100 crore at 1996 value. And it won Guinness record for the glare and glee.

She never knew that it was the canker in the bud.

Why did she do such brazenly stupid act?

Every man - from Viswamithra, the great to Viswanatha, the rank idiot - is a half man in presence of a beautiful woman. If she smiles, he becomes one quarter.

Every woman - from Jayalalitha, the great to Vimala, the gypsy - is a half woman, in presence of glitter of gold.

When decked in gold and silk sarees spayed with perfume from Paris and when a woman smiles herself in a big six foot long Belgian mirror, she becomes one quarter!

Over and above, the fertile breeding ground for superstition and astrology is the Brahmin family ambience – even now; even among top class scientists! (Ramanujan, the great mathematician and Dr Bagavantham a very fine physicist both were NOT exceptions!! Of course Sir CV Raman NL and his nephew Dr Chandra, NL were 100% rationalists!!)

These two- superstition and astrology- appear to have blinded a smart and goodhearted woman.

Where did she get so much money? Certainly not from her parents; nor from her savings as cine actress. Not from her salary an CM, as she had declared that she would accept only one rupee as her monthly salary for serving the poor and down-trodden of Tamil Nadu.

It was intolerable.

Every newspaper, TV channels were making "caustic" remarks and bitter attacks. The offices of a few media were ransacked; the officers who stood against her corrupt practices were not humbled, but cowed down by splashing "caustic" acid on their faces.

It was too much even for the very docile, rather insensitive Tamil Nadu voters.

CHAPTER 5

1996- 2016

In 1996 election, she was routed out and DMK was voted to power. Within few weeks, Jaya, Kanchana and a few others were behind the bars.

Jaya was in jail Dec 1996!!; It was not a movie set; it was real as bandicoots ran around the cockroach infested cell ;and the jail bars were made of iron not of wood or paper boards !! She was the first CM of Tamil Nādu to go to jail on charges of rampant corruption.

Busses were burnt and posters in the streets were torn and torched; all for a few days; but JJ had to be in jail for a month.

She came out of jail like wounded tiger licking her lips for the tasty blood of her enemies.

The craziest thing was: her stars forgave all her "sins" and realigned themselves during the subsequent parliamentary election.

Between 1996 and 97, the Congress party had become weak and the opposition party, BJP – Bharathiya Janata Party – had become strong.

Jaya was smart enough to "sense and feel" the voters' minds and she aligned her party with BJP.

During the election campaign of Mr. L.K.Advani a prominent BJP leader, a series of bombs exploded in Coimbatore and about 50 innocent people died. Fortunately, Advani escaped since his route was dramatically altered, far from the scene of disaster.

This time, the bomb blast of Coimbatore, threw out DMK out of glare in the parliamentary election and rewarded JJ and her alliance with thirty seats, out of forty. This meant JJ had got an extraordinary leverage to pull strings in Delhi.

Without her support, BJP could not form a government. So, it bent down to all her caprices, one of them including her position to become the Deputy Prime Minister of India in Vajpayee led BJP government. Never ever Vajpayee would have such nightmares!

Fortunately for Vajpayee, his government took a stern decision and his government crashed: what happened in next few months was the joke of that decade. BJP and DMK – the two arch enemies of decades – formed an alliance and forged a government in the center, which portended another jail term – perhaps this a longer one – for Jaya. Because, she has a track record of unending evidences of corruption to provide jail term any time, for any length of time What happened subsequently for a few years was the high drama in Tamil Nādu and Indian politics Jayalalithaa was barred from standing as a candidate in the 2001 elections because she was found guilty of criminal offences. Despite this, the AIADMK won a majority and she was installed as Chief Minister as a non-elected member of the state assembly on 14 May 2001. It was the "grace and benevelonce" of Fathima Beevi, the then Governor of Tamil Nādu, an erstwhile justice of supreme court. True, she was an honorable Justice; but an honorable woman too!! Only a woman could know the heart and head of another woman.

Within a few months of her taking oath as chief minister she became ruthlessness to political opponents, many of whom were arrested in midnight raids, her government grew unpopular. One such was dragging Mr MK out of his bed and arresting him in the midnight under the hue and cry and glare of TV channels.

At last she had made the venerable politician Mr MK cry in despair " Ayyo Ayyo"

It was a revengeful and spiteful act resented by the whole masses. This was her third big mistake.

The fourth major mistake done by an educated, book loving Jaya was closure of Anna centenary library, a massive very modern library in the heart of the city. It was an act of vulgar vindictiveness, something reminiscent of thugs destroying Alexandria library; with the same sheer vindictiveness the newly built Tamil Nadu secretariat was kept closed to rot and stink because they were built by her deadliest enemy Kalaignar.

In September 2001, she was disqualified from holding office, and forced to cede the chair to aide, a very good puppet O. Panneerselvam.

Upon her acquittal six months later, Jayalalithaa returned as chief minister to complete her term.

Subsequently, in March 2002, Jayalalithaa assumed the position of Chief Minister once more, having been acquitted of some charges by the Madras High Court. This cleared the way for her to contest a mid-term poll to the Andipatti constituency, after the sitting MLA (Member of the Legislative Assembly) for the seat, gave up his membership, which she won by a handsome margin.

After the first few terms of having been in office as the CM of Tami Nadu, JJ appeared to have mellowed down.

"Now on", she said unto herself, "I must work for the people and remove the stigma and stain stuck on my skin as an arrogant, avaricious lady."

It was during one such sunshine times of her career as CM, she had a strange experience which had unexpected twists and turns in her life.

Jaya could hardly stomach the scientific discussions and intellectual exercises. Though she was a voracious reader with well-set ideas about economics and religion, she kept away from science. It was not her cup of tea after all.

But today she had been forced to sit on the dais and inaugurate these scientific sessions, since it was an international event, well planned and organized. As the Chief minister of the state, she was expected to cut open the ribbons, light the lamps and say a few words of encouragements for all the organizers and the galaxy of scientists gathered around.

She did that very well. Because, her shadow writer Elan Devan, somehow managed to get someone else – a university professor to write the script for her.

The role of Mr.Elandevan was to make sure that the CM spoke something very relevant, just touching upon the purpose of the conference. All that was expected of her was to inaugurate, mouth a few words running into five minutes, give them her best wishes and then excuse herself as she had another important emergency meeting in the St. Gorge Fort, the secretariat of the Government of Tamil Nadu. She did her role very well.

The organizing secretary of the conference ushered her out of the dais, out of the gathering. All were middle - aged, well- educated professors and kept themselves at a distance, without cluttering her way unlike her party meets.

As she came out of the hall, she could see a big down pour of rain. It was a kind of summer storm, raining cats and dogs! When in Chennai or Bombay, it was never a rain; but a downpour as if the dark clouds hanging above have given vent to their stored, pent-up feelings. Lightning rented the clouds and thunders rumbled in the air.

"Madam, please do not step out of this hall madam. All the roads are flooded and driving the car under this thunderstorm is very dangerous. The electric posts may fall upon us or even the lightning is a major hazard..."

Jaya looked at everybody with subdued annoyance, particularly the organizers of the event, who had almost forced her into the inauguration caper.

She was literally fuming and fretting.

"Akka, please, let us go back into the hall and sit down for a while and you may take orange juice and relax for some time. We have to wait. Venturing out is too risky. After all we may lose half an hour. Not only that the persons of planned emergency meet also could not attend as it is raining heavily everywhere. You know this stupid Chennai rain! It is just very whimsical and unpredictable!"

"Like me ..." Jaya was kidding.

"Akka, you are unpredictable, but not whimsical ..." Kanchana smiled back. Jaya patted on her shoulder and both ambled into the hall.

They were seated in the front row, with two or three seat vacated out in a rush, so that the CM and her sister Kanchana could sit and keep counting the time to get out of this hot discussion, which they never understood and hardly ever cared to know.

As Jaya was sipping the orange juice casually, a few words came floating into her ears.

"This particular molecule, that I have synthesized using Friedel – Craft method has this molecular structure. This has been tested first on Guinea pigs, then on monkeys and also on some hardcore criminals, on the death sentence. Once taken in, it slowly gets absorbed and takes almost forty-eight hours. First it weakens the legs; the criminal cannot walk; then the waist. What is more when it reaches his brain, he will have a sense of euphoria, like walking on the cloud, like talking to the stars. He would be smiling and smiling until he dies. This is being seriously considered for euthanasia and also for the soft, suave execution of inveterate criminals!

In the beginning, such incorrigible cruel criminals were beheaded in public so that it acted as a deterrence for the future criminals, who were governed only by mortal fear! But, as civilization grew mature, we realized that we are manifesting and even nurturing the villainous cruelty within ourselves. So   death by hanging in a closed shelter became a way of getting rid of them; then came execution by electrocution, again in an isolated cell. We do not, we dare not see the agony of some other person, some other human being writhing in mortal agony. Now, in twenty first century, science gives much better solution. We get rid of the criminal in a softer, gentler way without having an iota cruelty in our heart; it is a sweet execution by a drug synthesized by our team.

What is more appealing , since this drug diffuses all over the body and gets metabolized, it is impossible that this drug has been injected at all. It will look like a quite natural, peaceful, pleasant end. No twitching of muscles; No signs of grimaces; no pains."

"Why did you discover this?"

Jaya blurted out in some sense of moral indignation.

"oh," The speaker, Dr Paranthaman was taken aback. IIe was ill at ease for a while; but bounced back

" Thank you Madam for this question"

"This drug is an amruth , a nectar, for a certain set of patients – particularly those long suffering by terminal, painful lung or liver cancer. They would die, with a smile. Death would be a happy welcome end for some of them ... like my father ..." his voice became choked

" oh oh , I am sorry, very sorry ..."

Jaya genuinely felt bad that she had unwittingly touched a sore wound.

What she has experienced casually got registered somewhere in the crevices of her brain. She could recall as and when needed. And she never realized that she would be forced to do that!!

"Akka", ... Kanachana   had been most of the time peering through the entrance of the hall to check if rain had stopped and rushed back to Jaya.

"Akka, rain has stopped and I had arranged for the security personal to keep the way absolutely clean and clear for your way to your office in the secretariat ... We may go"

Jaya stood up "Sorry I have go.. er.. Dr .Paranthaman"– prompted the secretary of the program, who was almost on the toes. "It was a fine presentation ... but I must be going ..."

She was ushered out by a set of body guards and Kanchana, always as a shadow of Jaya, slowly ambled out of the hall.

An important achievement of JJ which brought laurels to her credit was the killing of the dacoit Veerappan.

He was elusive for years together and playing cock a snook to all police forces of Tamil Nadu and Karnataka.

As his domain of activity was in the borderland between the two states, and had good connections and contacts with a host of "higher ups" in police department and also in politics, he could give video interview to the media; kidnap an old actor Rajkumar and hold him in ransom (which was paid off) but could not be captured. It was a real stupid drama, outplaying all the India cinema stories.

But Jaya was resolute on this score. Just she gave orders to the DIG Mr Vijayakumar, to bring dacoit Veerappan dead or alive. He just did the latter.

Perhaps because of all these, ADMK won again in 2011 Assembly Election and JJ became the CM for the fourth time.

From then on, the down fall of JJ had started

Between 2006 to 2016, for about 10 years JJ was sitting on the hot stove, sometimes as CM and other times as opposition leader.

You must have seen quite a few of Tamil movies, by Rajni Kanth, or Vijay. For about 10 years, these two would have individually acted as heroes in 10 movies, but with same theme, same stories, same fights, same jokes, etc.; only the heroine would have changed; yet movies went on as box office hits.

JJ's life and career were more or less in the same litany: she has to face charges of corruption after charges and go for one court to another. She would give hundred excuses, for not appearing to the court

Occasionally, Kanchana yielded and she went to jail for a while; then got released. It looked like that she could buy big chunk – if not the whole – of judiciary from the lowest court to the highest – including the Supreme Court. Also, she could find some ways and means of wriggling out of the clutches of law.

Fortunately for her, the strongest opposition party DMK, was in the weakest situation by its own internal family squabbles; perhaps because MK was getting old and the roar of the old lion did not go far enough!

It looked like a dynasty war between the sons of Aurangzeb, when he was alive and active.

The whole of DMK sphere of influence was divided into two regions: the north with the capital in Chennai under the 'lordship' of Stalin, the younger son of MK and the south with the capital in Madurai by the suzerainty of Alagiri. Among the two, the latter one was the rough and tough henchman, who initiated the sickening cash – for – vote strategy during the midterm poll in Thiru -Mangalam, in which he won with sizeable margin, solely by the muscle power and money power.

Adding to the woes, MK's daughter Kanimozhi was put into Tihar Jail because of her involvement in 2G scam along with a DMK MP Mr. A. Raja. She was in jail for 6 months and the later one was for 15 months, all due to rampant corruption involving few thousand crores, in the DMK cadres themselves.

After all JJ was not alone in scandals after scandals, scams after scam. May be this was the way of all politicians. When dogs and pigs wallow in marsh, who could be picked up as cleaner of the two!

Yet, a case filed by Mr Subramaniyan Swami, about 12 years ago came back like a giant king cobra. This was the case of "disproportionate income "as manifested by the crores and crores of lavish wedding conducted on her adopted son. During her first spell of jail for 29 days   the police officials   could seize few kilos of gold, silver ware, silk sarees etc. worth few crores. They all spoke in volumes against her.

The case was to be conducted in Karnataka, not in Tamil Nadu, as most of the judges were in the pay roll of JJ. An honest judge Mr.Michael D' Cunha of a special court, convicted Jaya and another three accomplices including Kanchana , for 4 years jail and 100 crore fine for the disproportionate asset case, as solid evidences exhibited in the luxurious wedding of her former son and subsequent treasure trove unearthed in her house in Poe's Garden.

Again, Jaya walked back into the prison and stayed for 21 days in a new jail in salubrious climate of Bangalore.

When she came out bail provided by the Supreme Court, she had decided to buy the whole pack of judges and lawyer with "tons" of pure gold and currency.

"Beauty lies in the eyes of the beholder" is a common cliché; it may or may not be true. But Justice, particularly Indian Justice, lies in the eyes of the beholder as proved by the way Jaya and her coterie were walking in and out of the courts every month and jails at least once in a year!

The glaring, obnoxious example was the verdict given by Justice Kumarasamy of Karnataka. He could twist the facts, enlarge the pinholes into elephant holes, close the gaping caves with stuff of rocks. This was in May, 2015

Jaya walked out vindicated of her honesty and innocence.

The whole India was agape!

However, her detractors, particularly Mr.Anbalagan of DMK, took up the case to the Supreme Course for a review. For about two years, the case was left to brood to hatch eggs at an appropriate time. All though this time, the control switch, the toggle switch – not the staggered type or continuous adjustment type – was with the Modi government.

These two years were more than enough for Jaya and her hench- woman! They were turning the earth upside down, bending and unbending the skies for 24 months. Supreme Court judge and senior most lawyers were shadowed, their weaknesses were monitored in a network of espionage system in every nooks and corners of Supreme Court -from the lowliest level to the highest level employees. Money was flowing like a perennial Ganges:

Where did they get all the money?

Every minister, almost all through her five term as Chief Minister, was chosen based on his/her capacity of "Tax" - the bribe- collection.

Do you have any idea about the " palayakkars" of Tamil Nadu?

Viswanatha Nayaka of Vijayanagara Kingdom was said to have organized this system in Tamil Nadu when he became the Nayak ruler of Madurai in 1529 with the help of his minister, Ariyanathar. The whole of Tamilnadu was divided into ten"Palayams" or administrative districts to be headed by the "Palayakkarars" whose duties included collecting revenue, administering the territory, settling disputes and maintaining law and order. The policing tasks they carried out was known as Arasu Kaval. They also kept a battalion of army for the King. (Puli Thevar, Kattabombam who revolted against the East India Company in 1800s)

I have just Googled off the above content.

Now you may replace Jaya for the Vijayanagar king and all ministers and MLA s for the palayakkars!!

There were at least four major resources for Jaya – over and above for the Tamil Nadu government. One was the big manufacturing units that came up in Oragadam, like Hyundai, Ford, Toyota, Daimler; all were finding Tamil Nadu a safe bet, in terms of extreme level of safety of their company, road and train infrastructure and availability of technically qualified work force.

The multinational companies would seek best blessing after paying through their noses, to Jaya, ten to twenty percent of their profit.

And there were so many universities, colleges, (both private and government). There was a price for each vice chancellor, professor, headmaster, lecturer, school teacher, DIG, SP, and attenders.

Everybody had a price tag.

Of course, there were quite a few who would not yield to money pressure. But many of them had weakness with women, alcohol and occasionally with hashish. It looked like everybody had a weakness; after all everybody has an Achilles heel!!

At the same time, after 2011, DMK also was in disarray.

Jaya made use of this opportunity and she had re-established herself as the invisible and invincible Queen of Tamil Nadu.

A number of sincere, genuine measures were taken up by her to alleviate the suffering of the people, particularly women, who unquestioningly voted only for her. Note, even Karunaanidhi's wives and Alagiri's and Stalin's wife would have voted for Jaya. All because of one single most reason that she represented the whole lot of womenfolk, who were kept under the thumb – no, under the foot of all menfolk.

The most important welfare measures, done by Jaya, all through her miserable days as CM, were: 1. Cradle baby system. 2. Amma canteen, water, medicine sachet etc. 3. Poor feeding in all temples. 4. Rain water harvest. 5. All women police station, banks, co-operative stores. 6. Allowance of Rs 1000 to each one of transgender person. 7. All school boys and girls got cycle, laptops. 8. Every house had TV, grinder, and 9. Poor disabled girls were married to eligible bachelors, with the Thali, from the Amma. And above all 64% job reservation to the down-trodden SC, ST and backward communities.

All these might be criticized as "free bees" given with an ulterior motive of winning in the election.

This is true; but only partially. Because, whatever be the motive the most important beneficiaries got the benefit!

When you find somebody hungry and buy him a lunch he will certainly would give his blessing, for you and your children for a long, healthy life. Whether his blessing will have any effect at all, nobody knows.

But his stomach is full and there is a radiance of relief in his face. This is sure and certain .

Jaya drew the praises of many luminaries all through her career: Mother Theresa, Hillary Clinton , the secretary of state of the USA, Dr Amalthea Sen , the Nobel laurate.

Yet, all these islands of good will were submerged in the sea of corruption, arrogance and high handedness.

Was it because of Kanchana, her shadow sister? Was she the Rasputin of Russian princess? Was the Lord Dudley of Queen Elizabeth ?

Many of the AIADMK party men of the past and present strongly throw the entire blame of corruption on Kanchana!

No, they are wrong; woefully wrong.

Because Jaya was not dumb, or half – wit. She was one of the smartest women of recent times. She had the razor – like incisive brain, to understand the situation, any situation in a coolheaded composure. The only occasion, when she lost her cool was, when she was mauled in the Tamil Nadu Assembly in 1984.

Just imagine, she was the only one woman, in a shuffle and scuttle of few fifty, filthy men all around!

Not only then, when she had gone home, locked herself all alone in her private cry too, she was alone, all alone!

Man can fight by himself with his fists, hands, and legs. But to expect a single woman to fight with a band of political rogues, with her fists hands and legs is just stupid.

She needed a gun!

The gun was Kanchana who came with double – barreled AK47, with full of –not bullets – but currencies.

With the brain of Jaya, with the hands, of Kanchana and her husband, with the support of all women – Jaya could become the CM of Tamil Nadu, the intellectual capital of India, for the fifth time!

From the day one, when Karnchana promised that she would live a dedicated life for Jaya, she did in letter and spirit.

For some strange attraction, Kanchana felt a bond – a mix of friendship, devotion to a heroine, and a motherly affection for a person haunted and hounded by a pack of wolves of men!

At the first instance of their meeting, Kanchana was just got flabbergasted by the grace and charm of this young actress. Soon, she could see that Jaya was a lonely, very lonely woman, in search of pure love and affection.

Jaya was frustrated by her father, then relatives, then the great MGR who would control her, love her, mold her, shape her, but never take her as a wife or at least as 'semi wife'! She has to carry a kind of stigma which hung heavy in the heart of a sensitive woman like Ammu.

Kanchana had to take care of all the roles for Jaya – one side as the henchwoman to kick out unwanted enemies, to collect all the ransoms, to monitor the "taxes" collected and to invest in various farms, real estates, virtual estates, to count the number of boxes containing crores of currencies. She was the Minister of external affairs, internal affairs, finance, defense, all rolled into one.

In addition, when Jaya was in tantrums, with over whelming emotions, Kanchana was there to swallow all the "Alagala Poison". When Jaya, was in depression, out of loss in court, or in election, Kanchana was there to comfort her, to put the iron -heart lady into her lap and bring her back to her real shape

Even Jaya, a woman of steely fibers had a knees-jerk rash act to submit her resignation as MLA, as she felt that she got enough of this dirty politics. She even said that for a hounded woman, like her, suicide was perhaps the only alternative.

Perhaps Kanchana was there mostly to restore the balance, to repair the marooned shipwreck.

Not only that in every occasion, she took the blame of the corruption and suffered in jail, more than what Jaya did.

It may be said that she and her family got a sizable property all because of Jaya and Kanchana's manipulations.

One must read the story of Roman war into Europe, or Ghazni's incursion into India, or Malic Kafur's outrage into Madurai. About one fifth of the "bounty" of war, "the booty" was always distributed to the army in right proportion; and the "size of the slices" dependent upon the occasions and the smartness of the foot soldiers to knight at arms and generals. Otherwise, none of the war, would have ever been won.

In a way, the role of Kanchana and Jaya was something similar to "Karna" and Duryodana. The former became a king out of nothing because of the patronage and friendship of Duryodana. Both have been portrayed as the villains against the holy

Pandavas. But, watch out, there was no parallels at all anywhere among the band of Pandavas, for the true, steadfast friendship between Duryodana and Karna.

So, Jaya was back in power and was sworn in as CM, on 23 May 2015, for the fifth term.

She had broken all records. She even contested in Chennai North constituency and won with a landslide margin. This means, the common people were all out for her, despite all the sins and the smartest swindles.

CHAPTER 6

Kanchana felt disturbed when she was woken up from her afternoon sleep, by the insistent phone call. She half opened her eyes to just see who was calling at these odd times. When she saw the ten-digit number, she became completely awake and her hair strands stood on the ends. It was a call from Delhi. She pressed the phone and glued her ears.

"Madam" There was a hushed voice.

"Yes" Kanchana replied. Blood started rushing up into her heart and head.

"Code word Jay kay 1471948"

"Code word Kayjay 2081970"

Kanchana 's heart was pounding

"Sorry Madam, Negative results. Many years of jail and heavy fine for everybody."

The phone hung up.

Kanchana's heart stopped; stopped for a few seconds and started pounding fast.

'This is going create tremors, earthquakes and tsunamis.'

She sat frozen for a long time.

Then she fingered for another number in her mobile.

There was a ring and a gruff voice on the other end.

"Sir,"

"This is Kay Jay 2081970"

"Okay; this is 2511950

"What happened?"

"You lost it, jail and fines"

There was some glee in the voice from the other end. The phone went dead.

She reached for some cold water and drank; but she could not become steady. She was so much shocked, so much rattled, as if struck by lightning, she could not think, leave alone cry.

Then after twenty minutes of walk inside her room, she went to the loo; then washed her face with cold water. Still she could not erase the face of fear from her face.

Something choked her heart; numbed her brain. She felt a certain total black out in the brain. Only thing she could do was to breathe and be alive.

Then she summoned all her courage and called for the driver. She rushed her car and the driver knew where to go.

It was almost four in the evening when Kanchana reached Jaya's home. Madam would be afresh after an afternoon nap.

As she knocked the door, and entered into the room, Jaya was dictating some notes to her personal secretary. As Kanchana entered and as soon as Jaya saw Kanchana's face, she could sense that something was amiss.

By the change of color of face of CM, the secretary stood up and quietly and discreetly walked out leaving alone the duo. He walked out of the door and had it slam shut. Kanchana locked inside   and then came near Jaya.

"Akka, we lost. I got the message from Delhi that the judgment went against us. He only said that many years of jail and heavy fine for all of us and he hung up."

Then I contacted the other higher source too with all our code words and   he too said same... She broke down and slumped down at Jaya's feet.

Jaya sat frozen. Her face went pale. She looked like a shroud, drained off all blood from her face.

She was about to collapse or end up with a heart attack. No, nothing happened. Kanchana was the first to recover. She stood up and hugged her, held her head in her bosom.

"Akka, Don't worry at all, we will overcome. We find some way out...."

Jaya became speechless. Nothing could she say; nothing could she think. There was complete blankness, complete vacuum, complete coma in her head. She blinked her eyes and that was only one that showed that she was alive.

She moved her hand and asked for water by showing the sign as you do in a dumb charade. Kanchana left her and moved to the next room to open the tall fridge, took out bottle of cold water and moved towards Jaya.

By this time Jaya had stood up and the opened her silver lined handbag and fished out a small golden beautiful locket. She opened it with a small golden key and took out a piece of chocolate kept carefully folded in a wad of plastic foils. She unwound the foils and shoved the chocolate into her mouth, smilingly.

"Akka, what is this........."

Kanchana had the sudden revelation that something was going seriously wrong. She lunged forward, dropping the bottle of water to prevent Jaya bite or swallow the chocolate.

No, Jaya knew what to do at what time. She lovingly tasted it then swallowed down.

"Akka akka what is this ? what are you doing ?

"It is a just a chocolate, sweet and tasty.........Nothing to worry...."

"Please bring me water"

"No, No, I am afraid, that there is something wrong. Won't you tell me even to your dear sister?

"Kanchana, please get me a bottle of water......" Kanchana brought another bottle and Jaya drank it very quietly. There was not a trace of sadness, rancor, or the pride, which were haunting her almost all through her life.

"Kanchana, I am done and I want to die with great dignity with which I lived."

"No, No, No," Kanchana cried in loud voice all of a sudden, it was in utter despair; it was a desolate, utterly helpless, hapless cry.

"Please give me that chocolate I will also die. I cannot live without you. I cannot think of even a day, with the pain of having allowed you die, just in my eyes,,."

Jaya smiled a wry smile.

"I have reached a checkmate.

I must say my fate has now cornered me at last into this checkmate".

"Please give me that chocolate for me too Akka"

Kanchana broke down, slumped down, like a wet cloth from a hanger, and cried and blabbered.

"Please, Please, I die with you."

"Please give me that chocolate. I had lived like a queen all because of you. Without you I am nothing. Only your love and affection made my life; otherwise, I am empty. I want to die with you....." It was mix of all emotions, cry in despair, blabbering of words and whimpers.

Jaya was sitting in her couch all alone like an aged idol.

"Don't be stupid. I know that you love me so much that you will never think twice to die with me. But if you take this "medicine" with me, both of us will have a heart attack in another half an hour. Then we will be seen dead in this closed room after our bodies stink and rot. The whole world will come to know that we have committed suicide. Never, ever two people will have heart attack together. But they commit suicide together. Everybody outside will easily figure out it. In a few days, the news will break out that we lost the case in Supreme court and the whole world will publish that we managed to leak the news in advance and so we committed suicide to escape punishment. It will be a big shame and disgrace for me, you and our party. Please stop this nonsense."

"If you want please take this key".

She threw a small golden key. "Take this go to Kumbakonam Canara Bank, Head office. There is a locket. Canara Bank Head office. There is a locket registered in the joint name of you and me. The manager knows that.

There is a golden box in the safe locker exclusively for us. The secret code is my date of birth. Open the box; you will find the same "Medicine". You take it whenever you want, eat it and then you will have heart attack after sometime, and then death. You will follow me after a few days. The whole media will respect you as a great, loyal friend of JJ, who died out of pangs of loss of a great friend. You will become a hero in the eyes of the party and also the whole world will really celebrate you as an idol of friendship.

Or you can take over the party as you know every nuances of keeping all the pawn and puppets of these MLAs and MPs; many of them are power hungry, money hungry and adulation-addicts. Maybe you and I all belong to this band only. Only difference is that I could somehow manage to move the pawn and bishops with certain shrewdness of mind and above all my stars have been in my favor all these times. Now, perhaps I have over stretched, over indulged in their benevolence and so retribution has come in. There is a limit for everything and I had tested the patience and benevolence of my stars.

I am done. Many times I had seen the stalemates but I was able to wriggle out every time. Now the check -mate has come in. I want to die in dignity like Cleopatra. My Antony was dead long ago and I must go after him, live with him, happily at least in heaven."

"Now go and get me a cup of Kumbakonam coffee and any of the books you can fish out. I want to die with a smile, a wry smile, like that of Alexander, like that of Cleopatra.....

Kanchana was utterly desperate, rushed to the next room, called for emergency doctors, ambulances, and rushed to make a cup of coffee which her bosom friend, her guardian angel was very fond of. She picked out some book and rushed but it was too late.

JJ had slumped out of her couch, like a piece of flag, like a fallen leaf.

In some cases, death comes as a blessing. It seems, retribution, comes slow and slow, but sure.

Even at the risk of life-long ill reputation, biting slander Kanchana proved to be a role model of true friend to Jaya.

Once Jaya fell down in her room, in Poe's Garden, Kanchana took her in her lap; cried bitterly for Jaya and she was ready to join Jaya in her journey to hell or heaven.

She got the whole landscapes of the situation within half an hour. If only she could get hold of the "Honey Chocolate" that Jaya swallowed both would go to the hospital and both would die one after another or even together. But this would bring big disrepute on Jaya, because any idiot would understand that both died by taking some kind of poison.

Two deaths by two heart attacks, even among the deadliest enemies or thickest friends had never happened!

Also, the AIADMK party with huge network of followers, party strength and enormous financial strength, would go into utter confusion and disarray.

Already their sworn enemy Mr.MK, even at the advanced age of 90 was waiting at the wings, like a hungry vulture, to prey upon the decaying AIADMK.

No, I must stand, live and make my Jaya an idol, a hero till her end.

And she did.

She called up the doctors, ambulance everybody in few minutes. Within half an hour Jaya was in Apollo, the most respected hospital in Chennai.

For next seventy days, none but Kanchana, could visit Jaya. She was so protective, so careful that none could break the barrier built by Kanchana.

None, means none, even the then Vice President of India Mr. Venkaiya Naidu could just peer through, (the glass doors) and see Jaya was alive and made sure that she got the best possible treatment.

For 75 days, there was hectic prayers and offerings, walks on the hot burning charcoal etc., by the "devout followers" of Jaya. Many temples, many churches, many mosques conducted special prayers to their own gods, to restore health and long life for Jaya. It was orchestrated in some places but genuine at least in many other places. It is the culture of Tamil Nadu. She was admired, feared, hated, but no one would curse death on her. Even her arch enemy, Kalaigar Karunanithi was full of admiration at her wit, and grit. He had admitted and admired openly; perhaps scared a quite bit inside!

What marked what surprised the whole event of seventy-five days of medical treatment in Apollo was the umbrage with which Kanchana protected Jaya under her wings. You could see the fearlessness and alertness with which a mother hen could cover all her tender chicks, when the eagle haunts overhead!

Whenever Jaya opened her eyes, which was occasional, Kanchana only was there to caress her in her fore head, hands with a tender motherly love. All because only Kanchana did understand Jaya's strength and weakness. Whatever was she, Jaya was her friend; and Kanchana was the devoted friend, who could willingly lose all her life, private and public, to safeguard and also project Jaya to the forefront.

In the story of Mahabharatha when Karna came to know that he was the first son of Kunthi and all the five Pandavas were his "half-brothers" or "quarter brothers" he cried bitterly; but promised that he would spare his valor against Arjuna, the only one who could equal with him in his valor and archery. Also, he said he earnestly wished that he must be killed defending his life- long friend Duryodana and also the newly discovered five Panda brothers. He did. He became one of the most admired characters in Vyasa's delineation of the long epic Mahabharata.

Kanchana deserves at least one tenth of such admiration for her true, unswerving friendship with her Jaya!

We must give the devil its due.

A few dozen Indian expert doctors from AIMS, Delhi, and foreign experts visited and examined Jaya. They could find that she was breaking down, cracking down inside. Death was walking into every corridor of her rooms, and switched off the lights in every room, one by one, something like the hemlock for Socrates.

Only difference was Socrates experienced the stages and stages of vibrant life and also death with utter equanimity. Jaya too. Because, she died when she wanted to die and also the way she wanted to die!!

For, she did play her battle well, very well.

Death was a blessing for her – a real big one –. She was given all state honors as she died in office as CM of Tamil Nadu. All the big shots, including the PM Modi, and arch enemy MK, and his son Stalin all paid their respect in due decorum.

At least, she was laid to rest in full honors, very close to her MGR's burial place. Something like what happened for Cleopatra and Mark Antony.

The final verdict that Jaya and four other accomplices were guilty came from the bench of Supreme Court of India only after the state honors of Jaya's death.

Death was a blessing for her – a real big one

Now is the time to quickly compare Cleopatra I and Jaya, the Cleopatra II.

"Cleopatra was the queen of Egypt (51 – 30 BCE) who influenced Roman Politics at a crucial period and especially known for her relationship with Julius Caesar, and Mark Antony. She came to represent, as did no other woman of antiquity, the protype of the Roman femme fatale".

I have just copied verbatim the above note on Cleopatra from Encyclopedia Britannica.

Just put the word Jayalalitha and period 1982 AD in Tamil Nadu politics, with Soban Babu and MGR in the place of Caesar and Mark Antony.

Note, Cleopatra was not just a beauty queen. She was well educated, a polyglot, powerful manipulator of the government officials, including the Egyptian and Roman Generals and Ministers. She learnt languages of Egyptian tribes.

When she was brought forth as a captive, Caesar just lost his head not only by the bewitching beauty, but also the grace, charm, the poise and the intelligent speeches she gave. He fell head over heels; and they lived together for a few years in Rome, until Caesar was stabbed to death.

At the assassination of mighty Julius Caesar, the Rome was in full turmoil and it was the best time for Cleopatra to creep through the fortress and reach Alexandria.

She had own enemies and friends. She was busy settling her score with her enemies and showering favor on her friends. During these two years Egypt flourished: trade and infrastructure development were done. Cleopatra showed, as a rare opportunity, to exhibit to the world, that she was an able administrator, with an incisive brain to grasp the gravity of every situation. Egyptian were quite happy.

Then came the bad news from Rome. Among the successor of Julius Caeser, Mark Antony outshone all others and was in good control at the helm of Roman affairs. Then Cleopatra was summoned to present before him, the role she had played in the assassination of Caesar.

Cleopatra delayed; delayed to test the strength and weakness of Mark Antony. Eventually she sailed a long path and presented herself in the attire of Isis, the beauty Goddess of Egyptian tribes.

Mark Antony fell flat.

It took few weeks for Cleopatra to explain Antony, in her bed, the causes of Caesar's death and her role in that tragedy.

But when Cleopatra returned to Alexandria, she was not alone. Like a kilogram of iron getting stuck to a magnet of two Tesla, Antony got stuck with Cleopatra.

And then on they became classic, celebrated lovers of the antiquity.

It was not just a physical attraction; because both had experienced sex a few hundred times from so many contacts. It was some kind of rare hearty love, each finding the next half in the other. She had the grace, vivacity, charm and elegance; he had the valor, stature and debonair.

In the heavenly love, they forgot the ground reality. Antony's enemy Octavian was boiling with rage in Rome. In the heat of hearty speeches, Roman's believed that Antony had pledged the whole Roman Empire at the feet of Cleopatra. Antony was "disqualified" as the monarch of Rome which meant the ships of Rome would and must move towards Alexandrea to capture Antony and Cleopatra dead or alive, the first always being preferable!

So, on a fateful day, ie., on Sep 2, 31 BCE the combined forces of Antony and Cleopatra were routed.

Cleopatra retreated to regain her residual forces back in far off Egypt. And Antony, with his band of dedicated army, fought and got defeated.

He was given a wrong information (whatsup was there at that time?!) that Cleopatra got killed somewhere.

In desperation, he planted his sword and fell on it to tear off his stomach and die.

When Cleopatra heard this after few days, she was heartbroken; head broken.

She just walked into her private chamber, took fruit juice, and then let out an asp to bite her and kill her.

She wanted to feel the pain, and anguish of her dear lover Antony.

The decent gesture on the part of Octavian was to bury them, one beside the other, like the grateful Tamil Nadu which buried Jaya beside the tomb of MGR.

Can we ever compare Jaya with other most influential women heads of the state?

Most of the "Kingdoms" had mostly "Kings" as the head of the state. Very rarely women were at the head of state or government affairs. Under this list of women came Elizabeth I & II, Queen Victoria, Catharine the great, Isabella of Spain etc. But note: all had a good fortune of being directly or indirectly heir to the throne.

Not Jaya!

This was understandable because the world states before 100 years were all ruled by brute forces or weapons.

Only in the recent times, for about 100 years, democracy was the way of lives of the world.

Even among the powerful prime ministers like Indira Gandhi of India, Bandara Nayaka of Sri Lankas, Hasina of Bangladesh, or Benazir Bhutto of Pakistan, all had great advantage of having born to great prime ministers.

Not Jaya.

She blossomed out of tinsel world of cinema, but was hoisted and fostered by the educated, semi educated, ill- educated and even uneducated women of Tamil Nadu.

She did not have the long legacy of party position as Anna or MK had. She could not speak Tamil in flowery poetic style of Anna or MK.

So, her only one strength was the common people. The only one weapon for her to keep all her enemies at bay was money, money, money.

A note on corruption or political favors is in order at this point: A person like Mr. Kamaraj was well above all this weakness because he was already an unselfish leader and all or at least most of the party men had grown out of Indian Independence Movement and for them the material benefits would not have blind spots . Not so for MK or for MGR. Among the two, MGR had enough wealth and he was by nature not greedy; nor did have time to indulge in corruption. But he has done significant level of political favoritism to let his lieutenants, knights win quite a few contacts so that they could fill their coffers and then build a fort around MGR and to supply money power and men power for the party, not for MGR. This is exactly what is being done by Mr Modi , the present PM of India .

But, Mr. MK, had a long innings in Tamil Nadu. He laid the foundation, fortress etc. for the Dravidian model rule with strong favoritism for different segments of non-brahmins, or Dravidians, who formed the bulwark of his "kingdom". In this process, he could have taken a few slices of the cake for himself too, during the distribution.

Without this, how could anybody, anywhere run a party?

Do you expect all the party men would devote their lives, without any benefit, for a cause - however noble it is?

A certain percentage of public money need be portioned off to run the mill grinding results.!!

Maybe the time-tested, tried and experienced advice had come from my dear Sir Francis Bacon ,the father of modern science and once the finance minister to Queen Elizabeth !!

He said pure gold might be shining; but useless; you need to mix some percentage of copper to make beautiful and durable ornaments and crowns!!

Corruptionless and favoritism -less governance does not and cannot exist. How much percentage of copper is acceptable in making gold ornaments depends upon how smart and honest is the leader and also how dumb and gullible are the people.

In Jaya 's case, it was a16 carat gold and greed was her ulcer!!

Another facet of Jaya was the description by poet Vali:

"Jaya was the saree-clad Abhimanya" who could face hundreds of enemies all around him. Yet, he would stand and fight it out, like a ferocious a leopard, keeping at bay a pack of wolves all around him.

Yes, Jaya did the same.

Whatever be the corruption and misrule that she had orchestrated she was a role model, beyond compare, for her indomitable will to win.

To the best of my limited knowledge in history, I have not come across a woman who had blossomed out from an ordinary soil, but was a venerated - almost deified - as an undisputed leader of a few million people for a few decades.

Yes, she died as a hero – not heroine!

EPILOGUE

Kanchana almost became the next CM but there were many slips between the cup and the lips.

Instead of being escorted to the Governor office for oath taking, she was arrested, put into jail, left to wither and wilt all alone by herself for four years. When she came free after almost for four years her sister Jaya had gone and forgotten !!!; the throne she left for her to occupy as the future leader of AIADMK has been usurped by the very grateful Mr Edapadi and his coterie.

Those days of Bharatha waiting for 14 years of exile of Rama was gone .... Gone with the Wind!!